In
Search
of
Beautiful

IN
SEARCH

of

Beautiful

DAMIAN L. BOYD

*Finding Glimpses
of God's Glory All
Around You*

XULON PRESS

Xulon Press
2301 Lucien Way #415
Maitland, FL 32751
407.339.4217
www.xulonpress.com

Printed in the United States of America.

ISBN-13: 978-1-5456-7259-4

CONTENTS

This book is dedicated to Damian Jr.
You are a constant source of beauty in brokenness.
I am your fan, and I am proud to be your dad!

Thank you, Joy.
Thank you, Denise and Janelle.
Thank you Emily, you are simply amazing.

INTRODUCTION

My wife Zarat and I were headed to South Korea to support our church plant there and to enjoy some time of refreshing. Flights from the United States to Asia are notoriously long and can be challenging for passengers. I like intercontinental trips, and this one was scheduled take between 13-14 hours!

We, like everyone else, filled our time watching movies, reading books, having intense conversations, and sleeping. One difficulty we faced was that we were stuck in the last row of the plane. If you don't already know, those seats don't often recline. Fortunately, we were spared a third passenger in our 3-person row so we could stretch out on the empty seat. It was still rather uncomfortable for me, although my wife, who is very small made the most of it. I on the other hand was struggling to find a relaxing position.

In my frustration I found myself wide-awake and looking around the cabin for anything interesting to take my mind off of my sore back. Since I was in the window seat I decided to take a look outside. With a shriek I said, "The Northern Lights!" My wife woke with a start and I allowed her to lean across me to see the Aurora Borealis dance playfully outside our window. I quietly refused to give up the seat.

What I realized in that moment is that beauty was happening just beyond my window. From my perspective I observed that I was the only passenger who notice the display happening right past the bounds of metal tube in which we were enclosed. People pay thousands of dollars to catch the slightest glimpse of what was a bonus for everyone on that flight. Sadly, everyone else was either too comfortable, to distracted, or too tired to witness one of the most dazzling natural phenomena known to man.

How many of us live our lives in the very same way? We can't see an infinitely beautiful God because we are too enamored with our own comfort, issues, and lives to see Him. I have discovered that more often than not, He is so near to us. If we could just change our focus we would be overwhelmed by what we truly long to see.

Chapter 1
GLIMPSE THE DIVINE

God is beautiful! All other beauty is derived from the original source. We can barely imagine how awe-inspiring He is in all His splendor. Everyone in Scripture that looks upon Him loses it, at His very sight. It is such a wonderful thought, that someday, by the grace of God, we will be able to experience that glory without the need of any filters. That image should make our hearts race and our souls long for the day when we will see Jesus face to face. He is where our search begins, He is the one who draws our gaze, and He is to whom we compare all other beauty.

Without a Christophany (Jesus appearing bodily) or at least an Angelophany (angels appearing bodily), we will only be able to get brief glimpses of the Divine. Can you imagine John writing the book of Revelation and trying to put into words what He was seeing in heaven? He was in exile for the sake of the Gospel, on the Isle of Patmos, during what was probably an amazing devotional time—and Jesus speaks to him from Glory. The conversation began with instructions for local churches, then shifted to the most remarkable invitation ever offered.

> *"After this I looked, and behold, a door standing open in heaven! And the first voice, which I had heard speaking to me like a trumpet, said, 'Come up here, and I will show you what must take place after this.' At once I was in the Spirit, and behold, a throne stood in heaven, with one seated on the throne. And he who sat there had the appearance of jasper and carnelian, and around the throne was a rainbow that had the appearance of an emerald."*
> *Revelation 4:1-3 (English Standard Version)*

WRAPPED IN LIGHT

We cannot treat an invitation from a Holy God as less than wonderful. Any time this happens, we should jump at the chance to be on His team, a part of His plan, and be where He is. There is no one like Him, and His invite overshadows whatever else we have going on. That is what it means to find true beauty. All other things become mundane in light of someone so stunning.

Revelation, chapter four is a glimpse into how strikingly glorious our God is: *"And he who sat there had the appearance of jasper and carnelian, and around the throne was a rainbow that had the appearance of an emerald."* Come on! The writer is doing his absolute best to maintain his composure. In first century language, John is trying to define the indefinable. He is talking about the most picturesque gems he knows. The colors are so vibrant around the throne of God that it looks like a rainbow, although it's like green like emerald. I get the feeling that words are falling short for the apostle.

The panoramic view is too much to take in. God is the centerpiece of heaven. We can think about eternity with God incorrectly, He is the one in the middle of it. We get to be in the presence of His all-encompassing light. We will have a new home, new bodies, a new earth to experience, and an incredible reward for what we have done for our Lord in this life … I get the sense that all of that will be a far distant secondary or even tertiary piece, to what we will be seeing on the throne.

John goes further to help us understand all that He is experiencing. Later in Revelation 4, we read of the thrones around the throne of God. Elders sit with crowns on their heads. That is an amazing sight to see, is it not? At the same time, there is a thunderstorm in heaven, but without rain. There is a sea of glass and weird creatures with a bunch of eyes, animal faces, and wings. John is taking in the awe-inspiring beauty of the elders, the glass sea, and the creatures, and everyone's response to the One on the center throne says everything.

> *"And the four living creatures, each of them with six wings, are full of eyes all around and within, and day and night they never cease to say, 'Holy, holy, holy, is the Lord God Almighty, who was and is and is to come!'*
>
> *And whenever the living creatures give glory and honor and thanks to him who is seated on the throne, who lives forever and ever, the twenty-four elders fall down before him who is seated on the throne and worship him who lives forever and ever. They cast their crowns before the throne, saying,*

'Worthy are you, our Lord and God, to receive glory and honor and power, for you created all things, and by your will they existed and were created.'"
Revelation 4:8-11 (ESV)

Then John is invited, "Come up here."

Is that not the least spiritual-sounding invitation? I love it because it is not about how this welcome sounded; it's about who the invitation came from. Whether John hears, "Come ye thou unto this special place," or " Hey come here a minute," who is saying it, means everything! If it is some guy on a corner, it has a different connotation than if it comes from a spouse. Whether it comes from the CEO of your company or from a cousin will determine the excitement with which you respond. A summons from a court of law gets a different reaction than one from a head of state. If the invitation is coming from the God of the universe, does it matter how he invites you, or are you simply happy that you received an invitation at all? Only the foolish reject a call from God. Sadly, we encounter fools far too often. Too many foolish people are blind to the incredible miracle of an invitation from the Almighty God! Let us look at the ridiculousness of a call from an infinitely beautiful God.

COME AND SEE

Sometimes the simplest things can change our world immeasurably. God's desire to let us play a part in His work is overwhelming. The moment a person loses their amazement at that simple thought is the moment they begin to wither away spiritually. Show me a believer that is not in awe of the fact that God allowed them to partake in the work of the Gospel, and I will show you a person that is either backslidden or not a believer at all. You may think this is worded rather strongly, and I would agree with you; but when it comes to gratefulness and the glory of God, things are quite serious. We must never outgrow our awe of God and His grace toward our wretched selves.

I am intrigued by how differently people in Scripture were called to be a part of what God was doing. Both the call from God and the response of his people fascinate me.

Consider examples in the Old Testament:

- Adam was created from nothing, simply because God wanted to know and love him. (Genesis 1:26-27)
- Enoch walked so close with God, that God literally said come here a minute, and Enoch was never seen again. (Genesis 5:21-24)

- Abram instead of a "Come here," was told go there! All He knew was that God would be with Him. (Genesis 12:1-3)
- Joseph received prophetic dreams that made everyone uncomfortable (Genesis 37:2-7)
- Moses was a murderer and a fugitive who saw a tree burning, but the tree wasn't burning up. That was weird, so he thought, 'I need to see that,' and God spoke to him from the tree. (Exodus 3:2-4)
- Joshua was told, 'Since Moses is dead, and you're next in line.' (Joshua 1:1-9)
- Rahab, who was a prostitute, received a knock at the door and God used that knock to welcome her into the lineage of Jesus! (Joshua 2:1-14)
- Samuel's call is special to me personally. He was a child who was awakened by God, and then God uses him to rebuke the head of the temple. He would forever speak truth to power. (1 Samuel 3:1-10)
- David was tending sheep when God called Him. Try to imagine what he smelled like and looked like after he had been outside with the sheep, yet God still called him. (1 Samuel 16:1-13)
- Nehemiah had a broken heart over the state of God's people. (Nehemiah 1:1-10)

- Esther was called through a beauty pageant (of sorts), of all things. Who would ever think that God would use the foolishness of a beauty pageant to call someone into ministry? (Esther 2:1-18)
- Isaiah's encounter with God looked much like that of John's; he saw the glory of God. He was so impacted by the fact that God would use him that His simple response was, "Here I am, send me". That is how we should all respond. (Isaiah 6:1-8)
- Jeremiah, in contrast, heard a voice from God and felt a touch, which he needed in preparation for some tough times ahead. (Jeremiah 1:1-10)
- Hosea had it tough when God called him to marry a prostitute. (Hosea 1:1-5)

The New Testament is just as interesting when it comes to people being welcomed into the work God has:

- Matthew, a hated tax collector and a traitor to his people, simply received a "Follow me" from Jesus himself. (Matthew 9:9-13)
- Peter was told, "I will make you a fisherman for people," by Jesus. Come on, that is a weird thing to

hear. But it was exactly what Peter, Andrew, James, and John needed to hear. (Mark 1:16-20)

– Paul is one of my favorites. The resurrected Christ stepped in His way, glowing and shining, and it blinded him. (Acts 26:12-14)

I could go on, because this is by no means an exhaustive list. It also needs to be said that there are different types of calls, and God often spoke to the same people multiple times. Do you understand, the point? God calls normal people into His glorious work and presence, and that is amazing! It is not something to be handled lightly or moved past too quickly. He steps into our stories to wreck us for every other purpose. He is a jealous God who knows that He is the very best, and He wants nothing but the very best for us. That is where we first meet real beauty, our first encounter with glory. We are given an invitation to know and follow the infinitely beautiful God; how dare we treat Him as if He is less than who He is.

I remember when I first came to faith in Christ. I was not raised in the most spiritual environment. I grew up poor and knew more than my fair share of sin. I knew, how horrible I was. I was even rejected by my earthly father before I was born. I didn't think that anyone of any importance would want me. Church was something to do, but many other people attending seemed just as sinful as I was. So, I didn't really want that. Church was a place to pick up girls who weren't as wise. Yes, I know, I was going to hell for that!

There was a moment, when all of my objections and all of my issues ceased to matter. I was at a church and the preacher was talking about blind Bartimaeus out of Luke 18:35-43. To this day, I get emotional every time I think about it. I understand how John and Peter were in the Spirit and saw things no one else could. I felt like I could literally see Jesus walking by me, and like Bartimaeus, I was about to miss out on knowing Him. I felt this overwhelming sense of dread that this could be my last moment to respond to His nearness. I fell to my knees and cried out to Him at the top of my lungs, and I didn't care about who was around me or what they thought of what I was doing. An hour later, I was not the same. I had met Him and He chose to come close enough to me and I couldn't resist His beauty. I was soon baptized and engaging in discipleship relationships, because I had met someone who was so magnificent that I was ruined in the best way. I was called into a life with Jesus and I would never be the same again. That moment lives on in me continually.

Without this first invitation, I am nothing, I have nothing. All must come to this place of salvation, glory, and splendor. Whether you call it coming to the foot of the cross, surrendering to Jesus, giving your life to Him, etc. It's a place of abandoning the ugliness of me, for the beauty of the one and only Savior. When we fall head over heels in love with Love personified, it changes everything.

I have had several such encounters with God. My second was right out of 1 Samuel 3. It was a year after the first call to know Jesus. I was sound asleep. I thought I heard my mom call my name in the next room. I got up and asked her what she needed. She, in her best Eli voice said, "I didn't call you." I went back to sleep and from deep within I heard it again; it shook my belly. I sat up on the edge of my bed and considered what was happening. The very next moment, I realized that I didn't hear one voice. I heard many voices. It was so many that I couldn't figure how many. It was immediately revealed to me that those were the voices of the people I was called to reach.

This, of course, was a call to ministry. I would be a speaker, preacher, and writer. God was bringing me into the work that I am now doing. But this ministry of telling people about His goodness started before this night session with Him. It had its roots in that first call to relationship, with my God. I wonder how many people are in ministry vocationally who've never heard the initial "Come here." Or they have never been dumbstruck with their eyes filled with His wonder.

There are some who would read my personal account of becoming a part of the family of God and being brought into the work of ministry and feel insignificant because comparatively, the stories are different. This is the beauty of looking to the list of how others were called: God calls us all in a myriad of ways. There is not just one way to hear God's beckoning. It could be a voice of a parent or loved one telling you the truth of Scripture. It could be through reading the text yourself where you encountered the God of the Bible. I have a friend that started her journey to faith by watching one of the cheesy Jesus movies that comes on television every Easter. Embrace your own unique introduction to faith and calling, but know that all are equally as beautiful because they all should drive our attention to the beautiful One.

Falling Down

The description that John gives us in Revelation is mind-boggling. It is astonishing to imagine the elders and creatures falling down at the sight of our God. This happens over and over again. The elders have crowns on their heads and they cast them to the floor in passionate worship at the sight and majesty of the Lord of the universe. I imagine that these stately elders are having a tough time keeping it together. They barely have a moment to settle down before the commotion starts all over again. They sit back down, they try to gather their robes and straighten their crowns and … they're back on the floor in worship of the most wonderful being ever.

For some of us, that may seem extreme, but there looks to be no sense of regret there. No one is wondering if all of this is necessary. Not one of them is saying, "I would love to be somewhere else doing something else." Everyone there is more than satisfied to be a part of this worthy display centered on the throne of God. They get to see pure beauty every moment and they have no choice but to respond in unashamed devotion.

That is what *In Search of Beautiful* is all about: finding God, whether in nature, other people, hardship, movies, songs, or even in books such as this one, and being found more in love with Him than you were previously. We can too easily forget how mighty, how lovely our God is to look upon. Our lives lose their wonder when we forget whom we serve. There is a power in seeing Him and having no choice but to fall facedown, just as those in heaven do. The sad part for us is that we have to rise and get to work, go to school, feed our children, pay our bills, etc. We are not fully able to stay in that place of awe, and that is truly sad.

What we can do is find moments to escape and behold His glory. Every day is filled with such moments. If we can train our eyes to see God all around us, we will feel less saddened by the lack of His exquisite presence. I wonder if that is the greatest challenge in the life of the believer—not sexual sin, not money or more stuff, but seeing God more. I believe all the things that so easily knock us off course are due to a lack of seeing Him. What if we grow harmful addictions because we have failed to become addicted to the King of Glory?

For some, this may be a new thought. For others, this may be a reminder of things you once knew. Either way, there is no loss when we find God most magnificent and deeply desire to see Him as much as humanly possible. That should be our pursuit. When we hear those simple calls of *come here* from the Mightiest One, we should be in awe, and run to Him. Whether a call to faith, ministry, or a simple daily devotion, it's He who invites, and that invitation should excite. I hope you will be encouraged to look for those small glimpses of our beautiful God as they are all around us!

Chapter 2
ALL OF CREATION

❧～⌇～❧

My wife, Zarat, and I find regular moments to get away. We do traditional vacations, stay-cations (a stay at a local hotel), retreats, cruises, etc. We like cruises because it gives us an opportunity to experience new locations while having to do very little to get there. We also love, to "not have to"—cruising affords us the opportunity to simply not have to do anything. Pools, fun activities, towels, are all provided. Cruises are great. I know that some are not interested in them, but for us they work.

We were on one recently and I decided to go on a jet ski tour. My wife is usually with me, hanging off the back with her arms wrapped around me as I steer the watercraft. This time she opted out and let me have my time alone. I was nervous, since the staff wasn't sure how much longer it would be safe to go out on the water that afternoon.

Apparently, you can't be on one of these vehicles in high winds and waves.

We were right on the edge of not being allowed to go, which would have devastated me. I really wanted to ride. We were quickly given the go-ahead and we were off. No time to waste. Our instructor mentioned that if we'd left immediately, we would probably be the last group to go. So we went!

The waves were so high due to the wind that this was an experience of a lifetime, especially for a thrill seeker. This was AWESOME! I was going five miles per hour over the top speed on the meter. I was getting a lot of "air" off of the waves. I started hearing this high pitch scream and was thinking, *Who is that woman?* Sadly, that woman was … me! Yeah, apparently, when I'm lost in pure joy I squeal like a little baby girl.

Add to that, I started spontaneously quoting Scripture while yelling, in the manliest way, of course. I was having a moment with God on a jet ski. Please understand that this was not my goal. My goal was to ride while feeling the wind sweeps over my bald head and simply enjoying the water. But, God stepped into this moment and made my heart love Him even more. The scripture that spontaneously erupted from within me was this:

*"I am the door. If anyone enters by me, he will be saved and will go in and out and find pasture. The thief comes only to steal and kill and destroy. **I came that they may have life and have it abundantly.** I am the good shepherd. The good shepherd lays down his life for the sheep." John 10:9-11 (ESV)*

That may seem like an odd scripture to quote on a jet ski, I admit it. The part that got me was that Jesus came to give us life, and if that wasn't enough, abundant life. I had walked through the door provided by grace and have been saved, so I get a life! Hallelujah! There is also a real devil that desires to take from me, kill me, and ultimately destroy my very soul, but Jesus gives me LIFE!

Let's look at the Greek to get a glimpse of what Jesus was saying. The word *life* here is *zóé*–life, both physical (present) and of spiritual (particularly future) existence.

Not just life, but life abundant, is *perissos*—more, greater, excessive, abundant, exceedingly, vehemently.

God wants to give me both life here on earth and in the future. Life is meant to be lived, and as I was enjoying the abundance in this simple and ridiculous moment on

17

the water, I felt His nearness, His personal calling into a moment with Him, and ultimately, His Beauty.

Moments like this are not usually seen as richly spiritual. But it was just that. I wasn't sinning, or out of the will of God in any way. He was with me, and enjoying the fact that I was enjoying this gift called life. It was a moment filled with His love in His presence.

When I arrived back on land, my wife was sitting under a palm tree looking out over the water at the shades of blue dancing in front of her. Bathed in sunlight, she seemed to not notice that I had returned. She was experiencing the same thing I had on the water. She was speechless, in awe, dumbstruck at the sight of the felt-tipped painted sky. I was brought back into that moment of worship on the water through the look on my wife's face. The two of us were encountering Beauty itself in different places, in different ways, but with the same glorious God.

LOOK AROUND

We don't have to look far to see glimpses of God. Creation speaks of our wonderful Creator. When you look up, you can get a peek at the one who said, "Let there be," and there was. How often do you look at the sky? What about the feeling of the wind on your skin or the sun on your face? All of these come from the same God who has a sea of crystal like glass surrounding Him. He made these things in part for our benefit and enjoyment. I love how the Psalm reads,

> *"The heavens declare the glory of God, and*
> *the sky above proclaims his handiwork. Day*
> *to day pours out speech, and night to night*
> *reveals knowledge." Psalm 19:1-2 (ESV)*

We all miss it on a daily basis. We can be so busy complaining about the weather that we forget who created the weather. The next time it is storming, take a moment to look at the light show in the sky. It is reminiscent of what is happening in heaven right now. Maybe, that storm is an opportunity to be lost in awe and delight.

When was the last time you looked at all of the beautiful colors in a sky with a sense of wonder? There is very little as striking as a sunrise or sunset. There are not enough colors in a crayon box to fully capture that splendor. Or, think about the fact that every sunset or sunrise is different from all the others and have been since the beginning of time. Wow!

Not to mention the mountains, valleys, trees, sand dunes, clouds, and the list goes on. The heavens are doing what they have always done. They tell us that there is a God and to look upon Him is amazing.

You may not like water and it may be a challenge for you to see Him in and around it. Then look to the hills. If it's too hard to gaze upon God through the hills, then see him in the ice and snow. If not the ice and snow, then fix your eyes upon the plains. If all of these fail you, then look out of your window, because it's there too. Caution: Finding God's beauty in nature is not the same as pantheism, which says that everything is composed of and encompasses God. The simple truth is that everything created came from Him, so we can see the marks of the maker.

You need only search for Beautiful to find it. We don't do it enough; it's the human condition. Our problem is not that He who has a rainbow shining about Him is somehow incapable of showing Himself. Our problem is that we too often can't see what He has on display. It's an issue of our seeing, not His being. His being has been and will always be. He is trying of to get our attention. What if we believed that God is always looking for our attention? How would that change how we see the world? How would it change how we see ourselves?

The Pool at Night

My church has a retreat every year. We live within two hours of several North Georgia Mountains. So, that is where we usually go. I'd personally prefer the beach, a lake, or a river. It's probably because I grew up in a small town in New Jersey called Burlington, which is right on the Delaware River. Nearly every day of my formative years were impacted by the beauty of the waterfront. As a pre-teen, I would sit on a dock and rock at the water's side. But alas, that was a long time ago and a great distance away, so our team goes to the mountains.

Our retreats are probably not much different from everyone else's. They are refreshing and instructional. A couple years ago, my wife, who books the retreats, found a gem of a place. It's large enough to handle our whole ministry team. There are picturesque mountains all around. The flowers were in full bloom. It is a really spectacular retreat center. The thing I love most about this location is, of course, the pool.

Once again, if you are not a water person, you may not fully understand or appreciate how amazing this pool is. First, it is heated. Then we can hear all of the nature around it. You can play music, but why would you when the crickets

21

and frogs are serenading you. God has a symphony all ready for us when we arrive. It has seats built within so you can sit inside the water without being fully submerged. It also has a weird shape that makes you want to explore every corner. Oh yeah, did I mention that you could see every star in the sky while floating in it? That is the best part!

Often we don't see the stars in Metro Atlanta. We only see the few that penetrate our streetlights. In the United States, especially, we have something called light pollution. Growing up, it was a rare moment when I was far enough away from the lights of civilization to see the light show that God had designed long before we ever had congested cities, let alone electricity.

I was able to see things on that mountain that I have never seen before. The sky was aglow with so many stars that I could not begin to count them. We didn't need all of the man-made light because the starlight was enough to illuminate the pool. It felt like I was looking at an image taken by the Hubble Telescope. There, in that moment, I understood how our galaxy was named the Milky Way. I could see the stream of white in the sky.

Stars twinkle. They actually twinkle. While floating on my back, I was overwhelmed by the colors that different stars twinkle. For the first time, the children's song made sense. I had never seen that before. I was lost in the moment, as I understood how the heavens declare the glory of my God! I couldn't see it until I was far enough away, still enough, and aware enough to stop and marvel at the display of light being conducted above my head. To think, it has been going on long before I was alive.

That show has never stopped. Like the one that John saw as he was invited "Up here," the sky speaks of the glorious One. It may not look like heavenly creatures and elders casting down their crowns, but the stars twinkle in the sky. Since mankind could look up, they have been wondering about Him, wanting Him, searching for Him—and I was joining all of them. I simply could not see that far above me before then.

That beauty was always there. The stars have always twinkled. They are even present when the sun—which, of course, is a star—is on display. The problem was not that the universe wasn't gloriously unfurled for all to see. The problem was that life creates a haze that hampers my view. All that was around me obscured those superb glimpses of the universe. In the same way, we can miss God's glory because of all the things that cloud our view of His amazing presence. We must seek Him who wants to be seen, but not until we can get away for a moment can we begin to find that which was already there.

Things too easily get in the way when we are in search of the Divine. We live our lives wearing blinders that keep us from being in constant wonder of who God is. He is ever showing Himself through what He has created. The hearts of those who love Him need only catch a glance to be lost in worship.

If we can get beyond our smartphones, tablets, television, electricity, etc., we may be able to see Him. There are so many things that interfere with our worship of the one true God. So many things vie for our affection and our attention, which is why I believe we must be *In Search of Beautiful!* The dull and ugly too often dazzle and leave us astounded at lesser pursuits.

What in nature draws your gaze toward our wildly beautiful God? How often in a day are you looking for Him in the small things around you? Vacations are too infrequent for you to depend on them as your sole inspiration, so how can you daily stop to notice the natural world and the God who created it? This pursuit is too important to leave to circumstance or occasional accordance; it must be intentionally sought and found.

Chapter 3
WITH GOD

I believe that Jesus Himself was in search of beautiful. He was in eternity from the beginning, as John 1 tells us. After His advent, He had mostly the bleakness of this world. Not that our world is totally bland, but in comparison to what He knew there, this is a sorry sight.

In one instance we find Him sleeping calmly in the midst of a storm. How was he not impressed? Maybe, when you have seen a lightning storm in heaven, the earthly ones are not so scary. I imagine He couldn't hear Himself think, so He told the storm to shut up! In another moment, Jesus even went for a leisurely stroll on water, in a windstorm that almost sunk a boat carrying His disciples. He seemed unfazed by the things that were vexing His followers.

What has always fascinated me are the moments when He intentionally pulled away to get with the Father. I find it interesting that even though Colossians 1 tells us that He (Jesus) is the image of the invisible God, He still longed to touch heaven, to encounter the beauty and the Father's presence there.

After large ministry successes, Jesus would withdrawal to a secluded place to pray. Prayer by itself isn't often seen through the lens of beauty, but when you remember who is being connected with, talked to, heard from, of course prayer is a major part of our search.

Jesus had just finished feeding the five thousand (plus women and children) after teaching them. He took this opportunity to get away and personally fill up on something more glorious than ministry service.

> *"Immediately he made the disciples get into*
> *the boat and go before him to the other side,*
> *while he dismissed the crowds. And after he*
> *had dismissed the crowds, he went up on the*
> *mountain by himself to pray ..."*
> *Matthew 14:22-23 (ESV)*

If the Son of God wanted to pray, then of course we should. Jesus desired to find that place where all else fades away at the thought and touch of heaven. We don't know what He prayed; we don't know if He was transfigured in all of those particular moments. All we know is that He either needed or wanted more than what this world could give Him.

Beyond the applause of the crowd, there He was in prayer. More than the satisfaction of a sermon well delivered, prayer. This is a great lesson for spiritual leaders as we can too easily live for the big moment in front of people, rather than live for the quiet moment with our eternal God. Greater than the joy of the miracle of feeding thousands of hungry and tired people, prayer!

PRAYER

Our personal daily devotions should be filled with a search for God's presence and glory. That is a special privilege that believers have; we have access to God. When we humble our hearts with the intent to interact with the Lord of all, anything is possible. We never lose, we always win, because we touch eternity.

Jesus shows us that it is not only in the regularly scheduled prayer time that we have access to God. We can have admittance to heaven all the time. Being an observant Jew, He would pray at all of the expected times, which would have been between three to five times a day. But apparently that was not enough. Neither should it be enough for us.

I love consistency, mostly because I have the attention span of a ferret. When I am doing the same good habits, it makes me feel mature and accomplished, but it doesn't usually last very long. I will spend time with God at the same time every morning for months or even years ,then something happens and I have the hardest time. During other seasons, it is in the early afternoon when I feel closest to the Father. In the first couple years of my faith, my experience of finding God was during evening walks. Although, what I have found works best is to check in with my heavenly Father as often as possible, regardless of the particular time or method.

Some may paint me as uncommitted, and that is fine. It's my goal to follow God into moments of personal devotion, whether morning or night. I believe the goal is to be with Him and to hopefully get a glimpse of Him regularly. There are some amazing guides to creating a consistent devotion; use them. They will help you develop a healthy rhythm of prayer. If someone else has painstakingly endured the frustration of finding a successful method that aligns with you, take it. What matters most is developing regular moments of connecting with God in prayer. Some processes are right from Scripture, and others are denominationally driven or even one person's individual method. The key is to engage your heart and passion in pursuit of the beautiful One.

My process is constantly different, and I have endured a lot of shame and guilt because it was not the same as those I have admired. I have been made to feel like less of a believer because my practice didn't match that of others. Once again, I have found devotional books and others' techniques to be wonderful in helping me create my personal prayer habits. But, I have struggled to make them last for an extended period of time.

When I came to Christ, there were an abundance of resources on prayer. One was praying for an hour. This was taken from Jesus' statement to His disciples in the Garden of Gethsemane. He asked them if they couldn't even pray for an hour. So, some thought that meant that everyone had to create a daily hour-long time of devotion or they weren't spiritual. I watched people wear their hour-long prayer as a badge of honor. The truth was, it was not an hour filled with prayer only, but Bible reading, scripture memorization, etc., which was not likely included in Jesus' challenge to His disciples in the garden. Ultimately, these hour-long prayer people were no more committed than anyone else. The people who adhere to the hour-long process did develop the wonderful discipline of enjoying time with the God of the universe and making Him a priority. Therefore, it was a success.

There was apparently some pushback from that style. Then, it was all about "quiet time": getting away from the crowd, like Jesus, to get with the Father. Honestly, most of that time wasn't quiet, because we (those of us who called it "quiet time") were busy talking. That was wonderful, but people began to forget that God is just as present, just as beautiful, in the midst of a crowd. But, it placed connection with God at the forefront of people's minds and hearts, so it worked also.

Then the jargon around our Christian conversation on prayer eventually moved to "quality time." It may not be a long time, or a quiet time, but it should be a good time. I liked that one! But, that seemed to minimize the vital discipline of consistency. Depending on when you began your journey with Jesus, you probably see your daily devotional prayer life a certain way. The one thing everyone agreed on is that every Jesus follower should have prayer as a regular part of his or her life. That is the point. Search, seek, pursue a relationship with the One who has pursued us. If it changes from day to day, or if it is the exact same rhythm everyday, is less important than the ultimate need to be with your heavenly Father.

Maybe, there shouldn't be any judgment based on how we conduct our prayers and simply ensure that people pray. This does not mean that there aren't solid biblical examples of how we develop a devotional life. Whether a person spends five minutes in singing to God, reads one chapter a day versus eight chapters of scripture, or reads from a devotional book, they get to know their Creator. Hopefully, all of these methods help us grow in our love for and our search for Him continually. That should be the goal. To help us in our pursuit, I have outlined some biblical ways in which you can strengthen your relationship with our glorious God.

WORSHIP

Worship is one of the most amazing resources we have in the exploration of the beauty of God in our lives. When we are making much of God, it causes our minds and hearts to imagine Him in all His beauty. I don't know that enough is said about how amazing worship moments are at inspiring us to delight in the Lord. Our minds have an incredible ability to dream and look for God beyond what is seen.

Songs, help us seek. Worship music is a powerful driver to the presence of our awesome God. Music has always moved us. Not only the believer, but also every human heart is wired for song. Whether listening to a funeral dirge or a party song, we are all inspired by music. Melody and lyrics pull at our emotions like nothing else. You probably don't have to think hard to find a song that would make you cry, laugh, or instantly transport you to the place and time you first heard it.

I love how modern worship music has begun to regain the power of the early hymns. Songwriters are recovering scriptural truths and marrying them to melody. That is what worship music is; it grabs age-old biblical truths and puts them to a rhythm. Worship music moves us past our current situation, struggles, and spiritual barriers. Find a song that helps you love God more and play it until your ears bleed. If it reminds you of how beautiful God is, then use it.

Psalm 150 shows us how music and dancing play a major part in our worship experience …

*Praise the Lord! Praise God in his sanctuary;
praise him in his mighty heavens!*

*Praise him for his mighty deeds; praise him
according to his excellent greatness!*

*Praise him with trumpet sound; praise him
with lute and harp!*

*Praise him with tambourine and dance;
praise him with strings and pipe!*

*Praise him with sounding cymbals; praise
him with loud clashing cymbals!*

*Let everything that has breath praise the
Lord! Praise the Lord! (ESV)*

We are supposed to give God praise in the place of worship. But also praise Him everywhere, with everything—with instruments, with dancing, with our very breath God will be, must be, and deserves to be praised.

Although music is a driver towards God, it doesn't have to be the only one. It is about the pursuit of Him who sits on the throne. Whether with knees bent or hands lifted, we get to do what the angels do … declare the glory of God! When I close my eyes, and think of John's description Revelation 4 and my own experiences with the Lord, I have all I need for my heart to want to be with the Holy God! Worship should be a part of our rhythm of life. Throughout both the Old and New Testaments, worship and prayer go together. When you do one, the other mysteriously comes along for the ride.

Bible Reading

The Bible is the Word of God. It guides us, leads us, and moves us closer to the One it's about. We must always keep the Scripture near when looking for the Beautiful. We would not even know what to look for without it. It's keeping us aligned. The Bible is a gift to us from God, and He uses it to whet our appetites for more of Him.

I love that the longest chapter in the entire Bible is about the Bible. Psalm 119 is a nonstop push toward valuing God's Word and understanding its role in our lives—which is, of course, beautiful. It has 176 verses that all center on the Word of God.

"How can a young man keep his way pure?

By guarding it according to your word. With my whole heart I seek you; let me not wander from your commandments! I have stored up your word in my heart,

that I might not sin against you. Blessed are you, O Lord; teach me your statutes!

With my lips I declare all the rules of your mouth.

In the way of your testimonies, I delight as much as in all riches.

I will meditate on your precepts and fix my eyes on your ways.

I will delight in your statutes; I will not forget your word." Psalm 119:9-16 (ESV)

Obeying the Word of God keeps our hearts pure. Purity is important if we are going to see God. We learn this in Matthew 5, when Jesus tells us in the Beatitudes that we are blessed to see God when we have pure hearts. Want to see Beautiful? Have a pure heart. Want a pure heart? Live according to the Bible. Scripture also helps us keep away from sin. You may want to read through this Psalm to understand the full benefits of His Word.

Did you see its connection to beauty? "Blessed are you" is right next to the teaching of the statues. Also, in His testimonies and the meditations of His precepts is delighted. That word delight is, *sha'a'*, which literally means to stare. It's the idea of being transfixed to the point of joyful satisfaction. We get a glimpse of God and it is exactly what we need. It's enough to satisfy. That is the point. When we learn to embrace, value, and lean on the Bible, we begin to see God through the lens of His truth, and we find Him marvelous to behold.

Like the combination of prayer and worship, Scripture reading should be a part of your devotional moments. Allow these three to come together in both structured and organic ways in your life and love of God. Pray the Scriptures, like in this passage from Psalm 119: *"God help me to hide your word in my heart so that I may stay away from sin."* These are all healthy habits to have working in a heart that delights in the Father. It is amazing how simple the search for beauty is, that we should feel a little ashamed of how often we miss it.

If you are having a hard time reading, use reading plans. There are more types than you could imagine. Some will take you through the whole Bible in a year; others will walk you through the Bible in chronological order (the Bible is not assembled chronologically); still others guides are topical. There is not one way to read it. Just read it.

It is not only necessary to read the Scriptures, but also to study them. You don't have to be a theologian to study the Bible. Get a study Bible that gives you background and context. It is amazing how much you will learn if you take a moment to look beyond the surface. The more I study, the more my heart delights. It's important to remember that the Bible was written in a different time, to a different audience, with different ways of functioning, in a completely different context. In our contemporary world, we may not be able to extract the full truths and meanings without tools to help us.

SILENCE

Silence is one of those spiritual practices that has lost its meaning in recent generations. We have given silence over to new-age philosophies, but silence should still be a part of our exploration of our Holy God. To be still and contemplative in a Christian world that values busyness and activity is difficult. When it comes to our daily pursuit of God, we must learn the benefits of quiet waiting and repose.

Silence is a position of the soul …

> *"For God alone my soul waits in silence; from him comes my salvation. He alone is my rock and my salvation, my fortress; I shall not be greatly shaken." Psalm 62:1-2 (ESV)*

I have had to develop a taste for patiently waiting for God. I used to feel terrible for my lack of silence. If I am honest, I still wrestle with this as a discipline. I am an extreme extrovert and find satisfaction, in part, through connection with others. It's the same thing when I am praying with our heavenly Father. When I am talking, or when He is revealing whatever He chooses to reveal, I feel connected. Moments when He is waiting to give instruction, or when I have nothing to say, can be excruciating.

The Bible is clear that our God speaks. Job 33:14 reminds us that God speaks, but we can be hard of hearing. Please take note that to some, the thought of God speaking is the most offensive thought imaginable. But, if we serve a god who can't speak, then He probably isn't God, and definitely not the God of the Bible.

Silence allows us to hear Him. My wife reminds me that if I am speaking, I am not listening very well. So many of us approach our prayer lives with a hurried vomit of concerns and worries, and we immediately leave that place with an "Amen!" We don't often stop, listen, and wait for Him to reveal anything. Silence and stillness are gifts that are too quickly ignored.

I used to resist moments of silence. My wife, Zarat, took me on a retreat into the mountains once. There was no television, no internet, and no people, other than her, of course. It was torture. Wait, I love my wife, but I like interacting with other people too. Maybe it would have been okay, had there had been a beach, waves, a water-fall, a nice pool … something! All we had in this secluded location were trees, trails, and bears. Literally, there were teeth marks from bears on our trashcans. I am all-in when it comes to trails, but ones with bears … not so much. We went on one walk and I kept telling her, if a bear eats me, my mom would never forgive you. Let's just say that forced silence did not go well.

In recent years I have taken on the role of a lead pastor of a church, and I have ironically started to fight for silence. It is interesting that with more stress, more responsibilities, and more challenges, I need more of God through silence. Now, for me, silence often comes in a crowded coffee house. I used to go to one coffee house, but a pastor friend of mine made it his place of solitude, so I found a new one. Somehow, I can get remarkable solace in a crowded place. My routine has been to simply find myself sitting still in the shower or before I get out of bed in the morning. In the quietness of my soul, it's just me and the Lord, my thoughts, and His thoughts (if He chooses to share them). The car also provides more than enough space for this necessity for me. It doesn't matter how you incorporate silence in your devotional moments, but it is worthy of discovery.

I once heard a pastor say that the true essence of worship is silence. I don't agree with that at all! When we return to that beautiful place that John describes, it seems rather loud, and I can't imagine a more worshipful place.

But there are moments of silence there, too.

To find silent moments, stillness, and reflection, is a Biblical principle. It's called *selah*. *Selah* (seh'-law) means to lift up, exalt, suspension (of music), i.e., pause. This is a common refrain in the Psalms, as the music would be playing during a great declaration of truth, followed by a pause to ponder that truth. This would be a radical concept in our modern worship experience, but it is a powerful way to not simply feel a moment, but to let your mind catch up to your captured heart. How many people need to allow their intellect to catch up to a heart on fire? We can too easily rush through life, going from one spiritual experience to another, with no *selah*, and wonder why we have little theology to quiet our doubts.

Finding stillness and quiet is one of the greatest challenges a believer in our technology-dependent culture will face. Our phones interrupt every moment with reminders, beckoning us to gaze downward into a world that can honestly wait. We have lost our attention and desire for the simple and motionless. It seems that our inability to see the beauty around us is, in part, because we are distracted by the glow of the screens in front of us. Maybe we will desire, crave, and yearn for true beauty when we choose to ignore the imposing imposters that have our continued interest.

REST

In our crazy world, rest is a dirty word. We are told to go harder, fight more, work longer, etc., but God never intended for that to be our total experience. The Lord made us with rest in mind. To deny the gift of rest from God, denies the benefits of that gift. This once again may be challenging for many, as the church has taken this world's way of functioning and brought it into our life with God.

Rest was written into the Ten Commandments.

> *"Remember the Sabbath day, to keep it holy. Six days you shall labor, and do all your work, but the seventh day is a Sabbath to the Lord your God. On it you shall not do any work, you, or your son, or your daughter, your male servant, or your female servant, or your livestock, or the sojourner who is within your gates. For in six days the Lord made heaven and earth, the sea, and all that is in them, and rested on the seventh day. Therefore the Lord blessed the Sabbath day and made it holy." Exodus 20:8-11 (ESV)*

I have found that this is people's favorite commandment to ignore. We don't have "sound" theological rea-
sons to ignore any other of these commandments. I have
heard it taught many times that the Sabbath is no longer
necessary. Some argue that a real Sabbath needs to adhere
to the old Jewish tradition of sundown Friday until sundown Saturday. Others take Sunday as their day of rest,
but most believers act as if they don't even acknowledge
that God wants us to have a day to restore ourselves and
delight in Him.

A day of rest can be tricky. In seven days, we are supposed to have one day of slowing down and being relatively
still. How are you doing with that? I have only honored
the Sabbath in recent years. I thought I was doing God a
favor by killing myself "proving" my love for Him, because
of my work. The truth is, grace made no such request. I
had nothing to prove! He could do more with six days
devoted to Him than I could with seven, anyway. It is a
greater show of faith for me to trust Him to do what I can't.
There are some wonderful resources on creating a Sabbath;
take advantage of them. Worst-case scenario, you get more
rest and a few things go undone. Best case scenario, you
not only live longer with less stress; spend time with your

loved ones, grow closer to God. As well as, stop sinning by ignoring a commandment.

As a pastor, having the same Sabbath day as the rest of the world is tough. I have to preach when others are able to come and listen. So, my pattern is closer to the Jewish one (although not perfect). Our church has also instituted a Sabbath for our entire leadership team. You cannot be employed by our church and not have a day to delight in God's beauty. We do our best not to call or require anything on those special days, except for in extreme circumstances.

If you can't get a full day, then start with a half-day or an evening. We were not made to go constantly without time to stop and rest. God took a day to rest, and we somehow think that we are exempt? Maybe that is why we get sick so quickly—in our more-sanitized society, none-theless. Perhaps that is why there are so many nervous breakdowns among church leadership today. So many of our highly prized leaders have heart attacks, strokes, or contemplate suicide because they are over-worked.

Not only do we reject the gift of the Sabbath, but we also don't sleep well. Science tells us that we were meant to sleep for an average of eight hours a day. We, throw that away as well. The longer we can stay awake, the more work we can do, right? The reality is, the less sleep we get, the less our brains function effectively. When we were designed, sleep was meant to be a major portion of our lives. Sleep is so important that we are supposed to spend a third of our lives doing it. Too many believers brandish their sleeplessness as a badge of honor. To bypass a good night's rest hurts us in the long run.

When we combine all of these components—prayer, worship, Bible reading, silence, and rest—we allow ourselves to see the Beautiful. We are positioned to encounter an infinitely marvelous God. Being too busy to do them is being too busy to see God. The truth is that, too often, we don't expect to have these moments of awe, so when they come, we can't see them. We are not looking for God around us. We should ever be in search of our beautiful God. He is always showing us His goodness and His glory, but we have to be aware enough to see it.

The consistency of a daily devotion, a day off, and a quality night's sleep allows us to find Him wherever He may be found. Every moment filled with these disciplines may not produce a "God experience," but they all have the potential to do so. In our search for the Beautiful, we can't grow tired of doing the simple things that bring us close to the wonder of the presence of God. To see God, to be with God, to encounter God—these should be the driving force in the life of a Christian. What has our faith become, if we are too busy, too distracted, or too blind to seek Him wherever He may be found?

Chapter 4

IMAGE BEARERS

❧ ～ℓ～ ❧

One of the most overlooked glimpses of God we bypass every day is the beauty in others. Pockmarked, wheelchair-bound, bucktoothed, deformed, bald-headed, too dark, too fair, too short, too tall, are all ways in which we devalue the worth of those made in the same image of our infinitely beautiful Creator. The vast majority of us are guilty of making judgments of others based on outward appearances. It's how we are socialized from a young age. Even those who lack sight find ways to discriminate.

This is part of the human condition that we must all resist if we are going to be successful in our search for beautiful. As a believer, we all have innate challenges that must be overcome if we are going to represent Christ. One of those hurdles is how we see and treat others. A core truth of the Gospel is that we all have worth. We don't get to determine that price. Jesus' death on the Cross established our value when He paid the ransom for our debt. We are all priceless treasures of the Lord, and for anyone to see themselves or others in any lesser light, is wrong. He is the remedy for low self-esteem.

Whether or not a person feels treasured is not the issue. Whether a person has embraced the power of the truth of the Gospel of Jesus Christ or not, doesn't change the price paid for them. The price was paid in spite of their acceptance of the power of what Jesus has done. He still invites all to a loving relationship with Him. Knowing that people would reject His free gift wouldn't change the worth He ascribes them. Too often, through our own ignorance and bias, we try to determine the importance of others and we sin in that regard, because we have no right to make those kinds of assessments.

It breaks my heart when I hear someone tell someone else that they are worthless, useless, or a waste. I believe it breaks God's heart, too. You may not have grown up in environments where these words are used. I have far too often and have been the recipient of some of them. I have even seen church leaders devalue God's creation, and sadly, believe that they are doing Him a favor. We can forget that the same God who created us, created them. He didn't only create them; they are a one-of-a-kind unique reflection of the Beautiful One.

Could it be that we have forgotten that the Scripture teaches us:

> *"Then God said, 'Let us make man in our image, after our likeness'... So God created man in his own image, in the image of God he created him; male and female he created them." Genesis 1:26-27*

When God created us, He made no mistakes. Everyone is a reflection of the infinite God. We are all image-bearers of Him; seeing anyone as less than that, robs him or her of personhood. There are some evil people who do horrible things, but that doesn't change how God sees them. We must fight to maintain that standard within ourselves if we are going to see and follow the Lord correctly. This is not always easy and it takes some discipline, especially when people act ugly. It is important to remember that even though people may be poor reflections of Him, they are still a reflection.

Have you ever met someone who is unappealing to you at your first meeting, but once you get to know him or her, you can't imagine anyone more beautiful? I know several people like that. That is probably because I often miss someone's innate beauty because of appearance or a personality quirk. I used to be a singles' pastor, and I would always laugh at the people who would say things like, "I could never date someone who (fill in the blank)." I used to just wait for the person that perfectly fit their "never" list to show up. That person was often exactly what they needed. They simply could not see the beauty until they looked hard enough, listened close enough, and quieted their own inward sinful saboteur. Only then did they get a peek at the One who made them uniquely beautiful. That small glance was enough to change everything.

RACE AND CULTURE

So many people in our world fail to identify the splendor of God in others. Oppression usually starts by viewing people as different; there is a quick jump to seeing them as inferior. Most racial and cultural issues come from the lack of identifying the personhood of another.

In recent years, we have experienced in the United States, wrestling with racial division. I would argue that the problem has always been there, but with the advent of social media, things emerged from the background. This country has a horrible history of race relations. As the settlers came to the Americas, it may have appeared as a peaceful neighboring, but in a short amount of time, the Native Americans were moved, abused, devalued, and almost eradicated. They were different and considered "less civilized," so they were not worthy to be accepted into "white" European society. And this happened even though many of those who arrived would consider themselves to be Jesus followers.

Slavery added to this dehumanization by creating laws that stated black people were a lower breed of human. This created a whole system of stealing Africans from their homeland and bringing them to the Americas as property. So, no longer are image bearers less than us; they are to be bought and sold as property. Now, instead of Jesus determining our worth, another human being owns you. How wicked is that? The horrible, detestable, repugnant truth of all this is that people who claimed to know and live for Jesus were some of the worst supporters of this broken system. Whole Christian denominations were created over slavery. God deserves better than that, and so do those who were made by Him. This problem is, of course, greater than white and black. It's a matter of the sacredness of being made in the image of God.

I have had the privilege of traveling to Rwanda, 10 years after their genocide. It was terrible! There were three major "tribes" in the country, the Hutus, Tutsi, and Twa. The Tutsi were the ruling minority class; the Hutus were the majority. There was conflict for years, but eventually, things came to a head. Seventy percent of the Tutsi were killed, and so were the sympathetic Hutus and Twa. An estimated 1 million people were murdered in about 100 days. I have held skulls of young children who were killed. It is said that more people died by machete than bullet. I visited a church with blood-stained walls where children were murdered by being thrown against them. In moments like that, where humans are being inhuman toward one another, it is difficult to see God's beauty.

That experience changed me. I saw how horrible we could be toward others whose lives are just as important, and just as valuable as ours. The most difficult part was, the Rwandans I met were the sweetest people I have ever known. I couldn't tell the difference between one tribe and another. They all looked Rwandan. But, viewing people differently than we view ourselves robs them of their God-given identity. I did have the honor of witnessing a whole nation's repentance and desire to no longer identify themselves based on tribal lines, but as Rwandans.

From South Africa's apartheid to Northern Ireland's Catholic and Protestant conflicts, to Nazi Germany or the treatment of Dalit people of India (considered untouchable), we have an enormous aptitude for dehumanizing others. It is neither unique nor rare in our history. When we look at others and fail to see their beauty, we are disobeying one of Jesus' most critical teachings. When Jesus was asked what mattered most, this was His response:

> *"You shall love the Lord your God with all your heart and with all your soul and with all your mind. This is the greatest and first commandment. And a second is like it: You shall love your neighbor as yourself. On these two commandments depend all the Law and the Prophets." Matthew 22:36-40*

Love God, yes! That is what matters, but he didn't end the conversation there. Love your neighbor. One of the best ways to identify your love for God is to watch how you treat others. We are told to love one another, care for one another, forgive one another, be kind to one another.

We are to treat one another well because it is of the utmost importance spiritually. Hypocrites say they love God and refuse to identify His presence in those made in His image.

The moment we begin to see people as "different" than ourselves, we immediately move toward viewing them as less than ourselves. Once we embrace that people are less than us, we have an excuse to misuse, abuse, discriminate against, or simply ignore them. That is why it is necessary for believers to see others as fellow image-bearers of our magnificent God.

My son is medically fragile and has some major special needs. He is mostly confined to a wheelchair. He is 100-percent dependent on others for his care. When he was about 4 years old, another child in the children's ministry at our church punched him. I don't know if that young man was feeling neglected by a teacher who was giving my son her attention, or if he was simply feeling overwhelmed. His actions reflect so many of our actions when we see someone that we deem different or less than us. He lashed out on someone he didn't fully understand.

Believing the Best

Jesus also saw beauty in people that others could not see. He was known for affiliating with the less desirable. The religious leaders were frustrated with his tendency to befriend those whom they deemed less than worthy. He was called the friend of sinners. I imagine Jesus wearing this title as a badge of honor. He saw people for whom He was willing to die. They were worth it! It doesn't mean that they were good people, well behaved, or even that they would become His follower. Jesus could see a glimpse of what we should be seeking, searching for, desiring in our pursuit of God. Sometimes it comes in the most unlikely of forms.

> *"While he was in one of the cities, there came a man full of leprosy. And when he saw Jesus, he fell on his face and begged him, 'Lord, if you will, you can make me clean.' And Jesus stretched out his hand and touched him, saying, 'I will; be clean.' And immediately the leprosy left him." Luke 5:12-13*

It was unheard of for a leper to touch anyone other than another leper. They would have to shout, "Unclean!"

As they walked by, so that healthy people could get out of the way. They were ceremonially unclean, and if a person touched them, that person would be unclean as well. Jesus, of course, was not intimidated by this man's brokenness. He loved and looked into the eyes of this ostracized man and affirmed his personhood. This leper most likely was alone and most assuredly went untouched most of the time. But, Jesus didn't run away. The Son of God knelt down and touched this man, and ultimately healed him from his illness. Jesus obviously saw this man's inherent worth. He was just as willing to die for this man, as He was for each of us! Worth, value, and beauty are always within view of our amazing Savior.

Our church is known for how we serve the broken, hurting, and neglected in our community. One way that we publicly acknowledge the beauty in those around us is by holding our annual backpack giveaway. Many of the school-age kids near our church live in conditions that will keep them from being prepared for the school year. We help students access their academic goals by ensuring that a lack of backpacks and supplies is not a barrier.

I try to be present with the children and families at the event. I am looking in eyes, I am hugging them, and I am doing my best to show as much grace as possible, because

I am acutely aware that people are looking at me (as the pastor) to see if they can catch a glimpse of the God that I serve. I am just as encouraged by what I recognize in them. I see God.

I remember one moment vividly. We were wrapping up the event, and I was tired. I had been lifting backpacks, moon bounces, tables, chairs, and tents for days in preparation. It was a hot July day in Atlanta and, quite frankly, I wanted to go home. We were picking up the last of the equipment, and I was stopped.

A young lady wanted to thank me for all of our service to the community and her family. The concern I had was that she was in a manic state. I could tell that she obviously had a major drug addiction. She was scratching and talking so fast that I had to really focus to hear every word. She began to tell me of her life in the streets, her addiction, her shame for the things she had done. This was not a short story.

At one moment, one of our church members had been trying to listen and gave me the "Do you want me to rescue you?" look. I waved that church friend off and just took it. After 15 or 20 minutes, the woman said, " I know what I look like, but you listen to me, Pastor. Thank you." In that moment I realized a powerful truth. She just wanted to be heard by someone who knew God. I did for her what Jesus did for that leper. I saw her as an image-bearer of God. I gave her the dignity of giving her my full attention. She wasn't too dirty for me to listen to, nor was she too broken. When our beautiful Creator looks at her, He sees her beauty as His child, regardless of her current state. Who am I to see her as any different? I finally hugged her and prayed for her.

Why can't I always notice people that way? Why do we all place blinders over our eyes when engaging with others who are hurting or in a bad state? It's not that they are bad image-bearers; it is more that we are not searching for the Beautiful in the lives of those whom we see as something different than ourselves. The reality is, at some level, we all are corrupt, wounded, addicted, and filthy. The good news is that Jesus still sees who we were meant to be and loves us in spite of our flaws. To catch sight of the One who sits on the throne means that when you perceive Him in whatever form, you desire to love that of which you are in awe.

To accept racism, classism, sexism, and other ways of demeaning human beings, is to admit that you have not seen the God of the universe in a way that has changed your perspective. If slavery in any form is okay with you, then I question whether you believe in a cross that proclaims the infinite worth of every human being. It is not that God isn't glorious to you; it's more that you can't see His reflection in His creation. He is right there, but our eyes are too dim to recognize it. God, help us to notice Your splendor in those You've created in Your image.

Chapter 5

BEAUTIFULLY BROKEN

S tained-glass windows have always enamored me. They are so beautiful. I am from the Northeast, and there are a lot of old churches with ornate stained glass. I remember attending church as a child (we weren't a very spiritual family). I could stare at the sun shining through the glass, and it felt like God was shining on me. Some tell stories while others have inlaid Scriptures. Even people who don't believe in Jesus visit older (or older styled) churches to gaze upon the beautiful glass. Maybe this is a foretaste of the Sea of Glass that is before the Throne of God.

Stained-glass windows are mosaics—patterns, or pictures, made by arranging small colored pieces of hard material, such as stone, tile, or glass. Mosaics are made with fragments or pieces of other things. Often, these are the remains of something else. Before a mosaic is arranged, it looks like rubbish. It takes a skilled artisan to create something beautiful.

Our lives are similarly fashioned. I am inspired by stories of hardship overcome by determination. Whether live or on the screen, those are the tales that stick. It is not the lives lived in luxury (although most would prefer it); it's the gut-wrenching ones filled with pure grit that grab at our hearts. It's the ugliness of life that opens our opportunity to glimpse splendor. That is where we see beauty. We need more awe in our lives, and I would imagine that you don't have to look far to see where it is necessary. Cancer, diabetes, car accidents, the loss of a loved one, the loss of a job—there are innumerable ways in which we see despair. But, if we look beyond the surface, we can still find His magnificence waiting to break through.

Add to that the fact that we all are considerably talented when it comes to bringing chaos into our own lives. It is so easy to proclaim our love and affection for our glorious God and turn right around and jump into overwhelming sin. Some have fought so hard to assuage their shame for these failures that they attempted to dispute the very existence of sin. We must own that reality, and know we are flawed and damaged human beings, if we are going to healthily search beauty.

There is always good news. Even though we sin, God's grace is greater! Jesus' sacrifice covers all of our sin, all of our shame, all of our guilt. So, instead of ignoring sin, or trying to validate our mistakes, we get to run to God, knowing that He has enough forgiveness for us. Yes, sin is real. It's so real that only Jesus—Immanuel, God with us—could deal with it.

We were so broken that God had to step in to save us. Over seven centuries before Jesus' arrival, this is what the prophet Isaiah said about Him …

> *"Surely he has borne our griefs and carried our sorrows; yet we esteemed him stricken, smitten by God, and afflicted. But he was pierced for our transgressions; he was crushed for our iniquities; upon him was the chastisement that brought us peace, and with his wounds we are healed. All we like sheep have gone astray; we have turned—every one—to his own way; and the Lord has laid on him the iniquity of us all." Isaiah 53:4-6*

He sees something so beautiful in us that He thought we were worth that sacrifice. He took on our sickness, rebellion, and guilt. Why? Each and every one of us has gone off course at some point. You are not the only one who has failed. I believe one of the greatest tricks of the devil is to convince us that we are the only ones who sin. But, when we embrace our awe-inspiring God, it comes with forgiveness for all of our sins. Hallelujah! This is the Gospel and it is as beautiful as the One whom it is about.

BROKEN LITTLE BOY

I have an example beauty and brokenness in my life every day. Some years ago, my wife and I were expecting our first (and what would ultimately be our only) child. We knew he would be named for his dad. I remember staying up all night and painting his room. We had all of his needs prepared for, as most expectant parents do. We were so excited to meet him, and I would talk to him inside my wife's womb. He seemed to be soothed by his father's voice.

Everything leading up to the delivery was perfect. We had no idea of what was about to take place. We arrived at the hospital with the highest hopes of meeting this little guy, the one whom we have been talking to, praying for, and bonding with. In the delivery room, we watched the nursing staff growing increasingly more anxious as they quickly entered and exited.

We were told that they had to get Damian Jr. out quickly as his oxygen level was dropping. By the time I was in the operating room, my wife was already cut open, and they were pulling our son out. He was blue, and that is not easy for a child of African ancestry! I watched slack-jawed as they resuscitated him. This lasted about a minute, but it seemed like hours. My son opened his eyes as the nurses rolled him past us, and it would be some time before we would see his eyes again.

The next morning, we discovered the harsh reality. Damian Jr. had a global brain injury and was not given much hope for survival. As a pastor, I am supposed to have words for moments like this. The truth is that I had nothing but tears and prayers.

My wife just had major surgery, so it was time to step up. For the first few days, I was the one at Damian's side. For newborns, skin-to-skin contact is necessary, so it was Damian Jr. and his daddy shirtless. I would sing and pray and rock my son who had tubes and sensors connected all over his little body. His father was his everything.

I found myself having to be his defender as some doctors were pretty much giving up on him. They assumed that we blindly believed something that would never happen. We understood what they were telling us; but as people of faith, we just didn't agree about the outcome. Indeed, it was time to become a defender of my family.

Most hospitals focus on the mother as the main person with whom to communicate. I made the medical staff call me as my wife was recovering. I wanted to know everything that was happening. If Damian Jr. made any improvements or setbacks, I would be the first to know. I was his first line of defense.

The doctors said, "He will probably never breathe on his own." The same night, I would receive a call saying he coughed out his respirator. They said, "He will probably never open his eyes," and "He will never cry," and within 24 hours Damian Jr. would prove them wrong. I realized that I couldn't determine what progress he would make, but I believe the best and pray that God would perform a miracle. That is exactly what we saw, day by day. We never gave up on our son, and he kept fighting.

Cerebral palsy, seizure disorder, developmental delay, and so many more diagnoses would be our future. But, those 26 days made a man out of me, and greater than that, it would "make a father out of me." [5]

My son is a constant reminder of how something so broken can be so beautiful. I find very little as beautiful as him. You can look at his little body and see so many scars, twisted joints, etc.; but when I see him, I see one of the most amazing creations our God has ever made. That is exactly the point! I see my son who is an image bearer of my God and I am in awe of the beauty. If someone else is too blind to see what is so clear to me, then that is his or her loss, not mine. It is clear to his mother and me.

God is always displaying His splendor, whether in the mundane or the magnificent. A person's perspective can camouflage what is right in front of them. It's our responsibility to find the grandeur in the shards of this broken world and when we do, we will catch a peek of the One who created it all.

THE CROSS AND THE THRONE

We have anchored our search of beauty in the Creator who started it all. The One on the throne is on the other side of a sea of glass, with angels and creatures in a state of constant worship. That One! That special One who exists in splendor, who is currently having crowns thrown at His feet because He is more glorious to behold than our eyes can take in. He is the same One who endured the broken state of the cross of Calvary. That is the best example of beauty meeting brokenness. Let's look to the ugliness of the cross to gawk at the perfect paradox that proves this point.

Our problem with the cross is that we have heard it so often that we somehow forget its significance. It is possible that you hear about the cross every week. This is not a problem for God; it is an issue for us to overcome. The cross was flawless, enduring, powerful, but we have lost sight of the glorious sacrifice. We never grow too mature for the cross. Once we truly embrace the ridiculousness of the God of all creation sacrificing Himself for us, we never get over it!

So how did Jesus do this?

Jesus, our Jesus, was taken into custody and questioned illegally by the former High Priest. He was questioned in an informal night-court session. He was hit in the face. If you have never been hit in the face, then you may miss the jarring nature of what it was like to endure such an assault. If struck in the right place, His mouth may be cut on His teeth, or He could have had a bruise or a busted lip.

That same night, Jesus was marched to Caiaphas, the high priest. There, Jesus had to bear the indignity of being lied on to His face. Can you see Him there? It is an outlandish thought, truth incarnate enduring lies while the beatings increased dramatically. The guards started slapping Jesus in the face. His face probably swelled as blood vessels broke in His cheeks. The Savior's eyes probably grew puffy. Then He looked up as one of His followers and His best friend denied knowing Him.

At daybreak, He was exhausted from being up all night and going through such an ordeal. He was marched to the Roman official Pontius Pilate. Pilate was renowned for his brutality. Jesus, being innocent, was sent away for King Herod to deal with. But Jesus stayed silent; Herod didn't get anything out of Him at all. Would you want to speak to someone that killed your cousin and whose father instituted a mass genocide to kill you as a child?

I guess Herod so deeply offended that Jesus didn't say a word, that he let his men have fun abusing the Son of Man. They dressed Him in a robe as a shabby king. This wouldn't be the end of that kind of mucking. Jesus was marched back to Pilate. By this time Jesus must have looked like an utter mess. His own people, who days before were proclaiming, "Hosanna!" or "Save us," were now screaming, "Crucify Him!" It must have broken His heart.

Pilate's men, in light of what Herod's men did, followed through with what they do best. They made Jesus unrecognizable. They beat Him mercilessly. They placed a crown of thorns on His head and the blood very likely streamed into His eyes, obscuring His vision. Then, being stripped, He was robbed of His skin one whip at a time. The brutality of it makes no sense, considering He was guilty of no wrongdoing.

Then they laid a cross on Jesus' raw back, weak from the whips and nonstop torture. He could only bear it for a little while. The One who was fully God and fully man could not carry the weight of it any farther. Another man had to be compelled to walk it to the place of the skull. Once he completed the walk up the hill, Jesus was stripped naked. We paint pictures with Him in a nice loincloth, but they wanted to humiliate Jesus.

He was laid upon the same cross that He was forced to carry with His bloodied and open back. Nails were driven through His wrists right below His hands and through his feet, and Jesus the Holy One was hung on a tree, which was a curse. They nailed an inscription, "King of the Jews," above His head in enough languages that most people could read it. Can you see Him there? It's not a pretty picture! Jesus was there, struggling for breath, naked on a cross. It is the opposite of what we consider beautiful until He proclaims, "IT IS FINISHED!" We can see why this is beautiful, because He finished paying the penalty we deserved. He had so much passion for us that He was willing to go to the cross so that we would not have to that is beautiful!

To see the sacrifice of the one-of-a-kind Son of God as anything less than beautiful is to rob the cross of its power! We were made more beautiful because of the price He paid for us. He who did no wrong became all of our wrongs so that we might be right. Glorious!

I love how Paul writes it to the Church at Philippi.

> *"Have this mind among yourselves, which is yours in Christ Jesus, who, though he was in the form of God, did not count equality with God a thing to be grasped, but emptied himself, by taking the form of a servant, being born in the likeness of men. And being found in human form, he humbled himself by becoming obedient to the point of death, even death on a cross. Therefore God has highly exalted him and bestowed on him the name that is above every name, so that at the name of Jesus every knee should bow, in heaven and on earth and under the earth,*

and every tongue confess that Jesus Christ is Lord, to the glory of God the Father."
Philippians 2:5-11 (ESV)

The cross is beautiful because of who died there and why. The One on the throne in Revelation 4 is the same one who is on the cross dying for the sins of the whole world. He didn't feel robbed of being God, to make Himself in the likeness of His creation. That is why so many are losing their mind in our panoramic view of heaven. The creature died for His creation. The infinitely glorious God became like His own less-glorious people.

He allowed Himself to be crucified, and there is the most amazing sight we can imagine. It is an eternal paradox that Jesus would become broken, and to our eye that would be beautiful. All beauty comes from He who is on the throne and won the cross. Wrapped in light and covered in blood.

I used to wonder why Jesus, after the resurrection, never healed the open wounds in His hand, feet, and side. He obviously was no longer bleeding from the lashes and crown of thorns. It seems that He wanted to keep the most amazing piece as a reminder to all that the most Exquisite One, the Most Wonderful Being that would ever exist, the

Brilliant One to behold, came to Earth to die so that we might not have to. So we could live eternally.

We need not look far because our God is always looking to give us glimpses of His Beauty. We don't have to embrace the darkness that wants to crowd out His light. He always desires to break through the madness and ugliness of our lives to show us His incredible self. We must search for Him, look for Him, and seek Him in our everyday lives. When we do, our world seems a little less bleak and we live with awe and wonder because we are privileged to see real Beauty.

This is not to say that we will always be successful in our search for the beautiful One. The pursuit matters almost as much as the arrival. If we seek Him, we will find Him— even if it takes some time.

The more we find Him the more our lives are filled with His presence and reality. The more we enjoy Him, the more we look like Him, sound like Him, reflect Him. We become reflectors of His magnificence in the world around us. As others look for an escape from their dreary lives, we shine in His reflected Glory. We get to be a part of someone else's search for the beautiful.

So … let the search continue!

ABOUT THE AUTHOR

Damian L. Boyd is a devoted follower of Jesus Christ, passionate communicator, visionary leader, and pastor. For close to 3 decades, he has reached and developed people both nationally and internationally through conferences, high impact events, leadership gatherings, and everyday ministry. He is a well-known speaker and has supplied people with the principles, tools, and resources to live significant lives for the Glory of God.

Damian committed his life to Christ at the age of 16 after a personal encounter with Jesus. Even with a turbulent childhood of poverty, homelessness, and an absentee father, he realized his amazing potential in Christ and allowed his challenging experiences to be testament to God's love, power, and redemption. He became a revolutionary for Christ and challenged those around him to life passionately for the Lord. His life scripture continues to be the theme of his life and ministry. "You are the salt of the earth…You are the light of the world…" (Matthew 5:13-15).

Damian and his family started Vertical Church (www.verticalATL.com), a family of Jesus followers "on mission" in the urban, college community of Historic West End/Vine City of Atlanta Georgia. With a mission to grow followers of Jesus Christ and equip them for their life mission, this Bible-based church seeks to have an indispensable presence and voice in both the college campus and community. Damian and Zarat celebrate 20 years of marriage and are raising their son, Damian Jr., a gifted, musical child with complex medical needs. He loves his family deeply.

In Search of Beautiful is Damian's second book; his first book is College Impact, Empowering Collegiate Christians for College Impact.

Contact Damian at:
www.damianlboyd.com
P.O. Box 965161 Marietta, GA 30066